BLS WORKING PAPERS

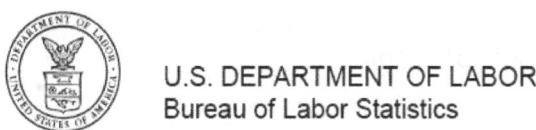

U.S. DEPARTMENT OF LABOR
Bureau of Labor Statistics

OFFICE OF PRICES AND LIVING
CONDITIONS

Higher Moments in Perturbation Solution of the Linear-Quadratic
Exponential Gaussian Optimal Control Problem

Baoline Chen, Rutgers University
Peter A. Zadrozny, U.S. Bureau of Labor Statistics

Working Paper 348
November 2001

The views expressed are those of the authors and do not necessarily reflect the policies of the U.S. Bureau of Labor Statistics or the views of other staff members. We thank David Belsley and Larry Karp for comments.

HIGHER MOMENTS IN PERTURBATION SOLUTION OF THE LINEAR-QUADRATIC EXPONENTIAL

GAUSSIAN OPTIMAL CONTROL PROBLEM[*]

Baoline Chen
Department of Economics
Rutgers University
Camden, NJ 08102
tel: (856)-225-6025
e-mail: baoline@crab.rutgers.edu

Peter A. Zadrozny
Bureau of Labor Statistics
2 Massachusetts Ave., NE, Room 3105
Washington, DC 20212
tel: (202)-691-6591
e-mail: zadrozny_p@bls.gov

March 21, 2001

ABSTRACT

The paper obtains two principal results. First, using a new definition of higher-order (>2) matrix derivatives, the paper derives a recursion for computing any Gaussian multivariate moment. Second, the paper uses this result in a perturbation method to derive equations for computing the 4th-order Taylor-series approximation of the objective function of the linear-quadratic exponential Gaussian (LQEG) optimal control problem. Previously, Karp (1985) formulated the 4th multivariate Gaussian moment in terms of MacRae's definition of a matrix derivative. His approach extends with difficulty to any higher (>4) multivariate Gaussian moment. The present recursion straightforwardly computes any multivariate Gaussian moment. Karp used his formulation of the Gaussian 4th moment to compute a 2nd-order approximation of the finite-horizon LQEG objective function. Using the simpler formulation, the present paper applies the perturbation method to derive equations for computing a 4th-order approximation of the infinite-horizon LQEG objective function. By illustrating a convenient definition of matrix derivatives in the numerical solution of the LQEG problem with the perturbation method, the paper contributes to the computational economist's toolbox for solving stochastic nonlinear dynamic optimization problems.

[*]The paper represents the authors' views and does not represent any official positions of the U.S. Bureau of Labor Statistics. We thank David Belsley and Larry Karp for comments. Forthcoming in <u>Computational Economics</u>.

1. INTRODUCTION.

Consider the discrete-time state equation and feedback control rule

(1.1) $x_t = F_0 x_{t-1} + G_0 u_t + \varepsilon_t,$

(1.2) $u_t = P_0 x_{t-1},$

where x is an n×1 state vector, u is an m×1 control variable, and ε is an n×1 disturbance ~ NIID(0,Σ), F_0 and G_0 are n×n and n×m parameter matrices, and P_0 is an m×n feedback control matrix. The discounted linear-quadratic (LQ) objective function is

(1.3) $v(x_{t-1},N) = (1/2) \sum_{k=0}^{N} \delta^k (x_{t+k-1}^T Q_0 x_{t+k-1} + 2 u_{t+k}^T S_0 x_{t+k-1} + u_{t+k}^T R_0 u_{t+k}),$

where $0 < \delta \leq 1$ is the discount factor and N is a finite or infinite horizon, Q_0, S_0, and R_0 are given n×n, m×n, and m×m preference parameter matrices. We assume that the quadratic form in (1.3) is non-negative definite overall and positive definite with respect to u. Superscript T denotes vector or matrix transposition.

The risk-avoiding linear-quadratic-exponential-Gaussian (LQEG) objective function is

(1.4) $J(x_{t-1},N) = E_{t-1}\exp[-v(x_{t-1},N)],$

where E_{t-1} denotes expectation conditioned on variables realized in period t-1. The discrete-time LQEG problem is: given x_{t-1}, N, and the parameters F_0, G_0, Σ, R_0, S_0, and Q_0, minimize (1.4) with respect to P_0, subject to (1.1) to (1.3).

Jacobson (1973) showed that, for finite N, the optimal P_0 is obtained by iterating on a discrete-time recursive Riccati equation. As N → ∞, the equation converges to a nonrecursive or algebraic Riccati equation, which can be solved quickly and accurately using the Schur-decomposition method (Laub, 1979). See also Hansen and Sargent (1995). Karp (1985) addressed the problem of determining the contribution of higher moments (> 2) of ε to the value of the LQEG objective function, $J(x_{t-1},N)$. Expanding $J(x_{t-1},N)$ in a Taylor-series and using some matrix differentiation rules of MacRae (1974), Karp derived an algorithm for computing a two-term approximation of $J(x_{t-1}, N)$ based on the 2nd and 4th moments of ε (odd moments of ε are zero). The complexity of MacRae's differentiation rules apparently dissuaded Karp from attempting to derive equations for computing higher-order (> 2) terms based on higher moments (> 4) of ε.

The present paper extends Karp's results in two ways. First, using a simpler representation of matrix derivatives based on the total-differential rather than on partial-derivative forms (Magnus and Neudecker, 1988), the paper derives a simple recursion for computing any moments of a Gaussian random vector. Second, using this result, the paper applies the perturbation method (Judd, 1998, chs. 13-14) to derive equations for computing the 4th-order Taylor-series approximation of $J(x_{t-1}, \infty)$, based on the 2nd and 4th moments of ε. The second result illustrates using higher Gaussian moments in a perturbation solution of a nonlinear dynamic stochastic model. There is a growing interest in economics in solving dynamic stochastic models with the perturbation method (Anderson and Hansen, 1996; Chen and Zadrozny, 2000b; Collard and Juillard, 2000; Sims, 2000).

The paper proceeds as follows. Section 2 states and proves a theorem and corollary that give the recursion for computing any multivariate Gaussian moment. Section 3 derives linear, perturbation-solution equations for computing the 4th-order approximation of $J(x_{t-1}, \infty)$ for the undiscounted problem. Section 4 illustrates the results of Section 3 numerically. Section 5 gives concluding remarks. There are two technical appendices. Appendix A explains the definitions and rules of matrix differentiation that are used in Sections 2 and 3. Appendix B explains how to compute the 1st- to 4th-order derivatives of $f(x) = \exp[-(1/2)x^T Q x]$, in the gradient forms defined in appendix A, that are inputs in the perturbation solution equations of Section 3.

2. RECURSION FOR COMPUTING ANY MULTIVARIATE GAUSSIAN MOMENT.

This section follows the definitions and rules of matrix differentiation explained in appendix A, which the reader should read before proceeding.

Let x be a random n-vector distributed $N(\mu, \Sigma)$ and let $m(z) = E[\exp(x^T z)]$, for $z \in \mathbf{R}^n$, be its moment generating function given by

$$(2.1) \qquad m(z) = \exp[\mu^T z + (1/2) z^T \Sigma z].$$

As explained in appendix A, $\nabla^k m(z)$ is the kth-order gradient matrix of kth-order partial derivatives of $m(z)$. Let μ_k be the kth uncentered moment of x defined as $\mu_k = E(\Pi_k \otimes x)$, where $\Pi_k \otimes x$ denotes k-1 successive Kronecker products of x (e.g., $\Pi_2 \otimes x = x \otimes x$). Then, $\mu_k = \text{vec}[\nabla^k m(0)]$. The following theorem states a recursion for computing $\nabla^k m(z)$ for any finite k.

THEOREM 1: Suppose $x \in \mathbf{R}^n \sim N(\mu, \Sigma)$, with moment generating function $m(z)$ given by (2.1). Then, for $k = 3, \ldots, K$,

$$(2.2) \qquad \text{vec}[\nabla^k m(z)] = \text{vec}\{[\nabla^{k-1} m(z)^T \otimes (\mu + \Sigma z)] + (k-1)[\nabla^{k-2} m(z)^T \otimes \Sigma)]\},$$

where $\nabla^k m(z)$ is $n^{k-1} \times n$, starting with $\nabla m(z) = m(z)(\mu^T + z^T \Sigma)$ and $\nabla^2 m(z) = (\mu + \Sigma z)\nabla m(z) + m(z)\Sigma$.

Theorem 1 immediately implies

COROLLARY 1: For $k = 3, \ldots, K$,

$$(2.3) \qquad \mu_k = \text{vec}\{[\text{mat}(\mu_{k-1})^T \otimes \mu] + (k-1)[\text{mat}(\mu_{k-2})^T \otimes \Sigma]\},$$

starting with $\mu_1 = \mu$ and $\mu_2 = (\mu \otimes \mu) + \text{vec}(\Sigma)$, where $\text{mat}(\mu_k)$ denotes the unvectorization of μ_k to an $n^{k-1} \times n$ dimensional matrix.

There is a subtlety in the role of the vectorization operator in (2.3). One might think we could unvectorize (2.3) and write it as $\text{mat}(\mu_k) = [\text{mat}(\mu_{k-1})^T \otimes \mu] + (k-1)[\text{mat}(\mu_{k-2})^T \otimes \Sigma]$, but this cannot be done because, whereas $\text{mat}(\mu_k)$ is $n^{k-1} \times n$, $[\text{mat}(\mu_{k-1})^T \otimes \mu] + (k-1)[\text{mat}(\mu_{k-2})^T \otimes \Sigma]$ is $n^2 \times n^{k-2}$.

Corollary 1 is the principal result of this section. For $k = 4$, (2.3) corresponds to Karp's (1985) equation (10), based on MacRae's (1974) definition of a matrix derivative. Whereas (2.3) is valid for any k, it would be very tedious to extend Karp's equation (10) correspondingly. We now prove theorem 1.

PROOF OF THEOREM 1:

We repeatedly vectorize and differentiate expressions by applying rules (A.3), (A.19), and (A.20), without referencing them explicitly. We also repeatedly use the fact that $m(z)$ is a scalar.

1. Derivation of $\nabla m(z)$: Differentiating (2.1), we obtain

$$(2.4) \qquad dm(z) = m(z)(\mu^T + z^T\Sigma)dz.$$

Then, because $dm(z) = \nabla m(z)dz$ holds for all dz, we can drop dz and obtain $\nabla m(z) = m(z)(\mu^T + z^T\Sigma)$.

2. Derivation of $\nabla^2 m(z)$: Differentiating (2.4) and vectorizing terms, we obtain

$$(2.5) \qquad d^2m(z) = dm(z)(\mu^T + z^T\Sigma)dz + m(z)dz^T\Sigma dz$$

$$= dz^T[(\mu + \Sigma z)dm(z) + m(z)\Sigma dz]$$

$$= dz^T[(\mu + \Sigma z)\nabla m(z) + m(z)\Sigma]dz.$$

Then, because $d^2m(z) = dz^T\nabla m(z)dz$ holds for all dz, we can drop dz and obtain $\nabla^2 m(z) = (\mu + \Sigma z)\nabla m(z) + m(z)\Sigma$.

3. Derivation of (2.2) for $k = 3$: Differentiating (2.5) and vectorizing terms, we obtain

$$(2.6) \qquad d^3m(z) = d^2m(z)(\mu^T + z^T\Sigma)dz + 2dm(z)dz^T\Sigma dz$$

$$= dz^T[(\mu + \Sigma z)d^2m(z) + 2\Sigma dz dm(z)]$$

$$= dz^T[(\mu + \Sigma z)dz^T\nabla^2 m(z) + 2\Sigma dz\nabla m(z)]dz$$

$$= (\Pi_2\otimes dz^T)\text{vec}[(\mu + \Sigma z)dz^T\nabla^2 m(z) + 2\Sigma dz\nabla m(z)]$$

$$= (\Pi_2\otimes dz^T)\{[\nabla^2 m(z)^T \otimes (\mu + \Sigma z)] + 2[\nabla m(z)^T \otimes \Sigma]\}dz.$$

Then, because $d^3m(z) = (\Pi_2\otimes dz^T)\nabla^3 m(z)dz$ holds for all dz, we can drop dz and obtain $\nabla^3 m(z) = [\nabla^2 m(z)^T \otimes (\mu + \Sigma z)] + 2[\nabla m(z)^T \otimes \Sigma]$.

4. Derivation of (2.2) for $k = 4$: Differentiating (2.6) and vectorizing terms, we obtain

$$(2.7) \qquad d^4 m(z) = d^3 m(z)(\mu^T + z^T \Sigma) dz + 3 d^2 m(z) dz^T \Sigma dz$$

$$= dz^T[(\mu + \Sigma z) d^3 m(z) + 3\Sigma dz d^2 m(z)]$$

$$= dz^T[(\mu + \Sigma z)(\Pi_2 \otimes dz^T) \nabla^3 m(z) + 3\Sigma dz dz^T \nabla^2 m(z)] dz$$

$$= (\Pi_2 \otimes dz^T) vec[(\mu + \Sigma z)(\Pi_2 \otimes dz^T) \nabla^3 m(z) + 3\Sigma dz dz^T \nabla^2 m(z)]$$

$$= (\Pi_2 \otimes dz^T)\{[\nabla^3 m(z)^T \otimes (\mu + \Sigma z)] + 3[\nabla^2 m(z)^T \otimes \Sigma]\}(\Pi_2 \otimes dz)$$

$$= (\Pi_4 \otimes dz^T) vec\{[\nabla^3 m(z)^T \otimes (\mu + \Sigma z)] + 3[\nabla^2 m(z)^T \otimes \Sigma]\}.$$

Then, because $d^4 m(z) = (\Pi_3 \otimes dz^T) \nabla^3 m(z) dz = (\Pi_4 \otimes dz^T) vec[\nabla^3 m(z)]$ holds for all dz, we can drop dz and obtain $vec[\nabla^4 m(z)] = vec\{[\nabla^3 m(z)^T \otimes (\mu + \Sigma z)] + 3[\nabla^2 m(z)^T \otimes \Sigma]\}$.

    5. Derivation of (2.2) for $k \geq 5$: Continuing in this fashion,

$$(2.8) \qquad d^k m(z) = d^{k-1} m(z)(\mu^T + z^T \Sigma) dz + (k-1) d^{k-2} m(z) dz^T \Sigma dz$$

$$= dz^T[(\mu + \Sigma z) d^{k-1} m(z) + (k-1)\Sigma dz d^{k-2} m(z)]$$

$$= dz^T[(\mu + \Sigma z)(\Pi_{k-2} \otimes dz^T) \nabla^{k-1} m(z) + (k-1)\Sigma dz (\Pi_{k-3} \otimes dz^T) \nabla^{k-2} m(z)] dz$$

$$= (\Pi_2 \otimes dz^T) vec[(\mu + \Sigma z)(\Pi_{k-2} \otimes dz^T) \nabla^{k-1} m(z) + (k-1)\Sigma dz (\Pi_{k-3} \otimes dz^T) \nabla^{k-2} m(z)]$$

$$= (\Pi_2 \otimes dz^T)\{[\nabla^{k-1} m(z)^T \otimes (\mu + \Sigma z)] + (k-1)[\nabla^{k-2} m(z)^T \otimes \Sigma]\}(\Pi_{k-2} \otimes dz)$$

$$= (\Pi_k \otimes dz^T) vec\{[\nabla^{k-1} m(z)^T \otimes (\mu + \Sigma z)] + (k-1)[\nabla^{k-2} m(z)^T \otimes \Sigma]\}.$$

Then, because $d^k m(z) = (\Pi_k \otimes dz^T) vec[\nabla^k m(z)]$ holds for all dz, we can drop dz and obtain $vec[\nabla^k m(z)] = vec\{[\nabla^{k-1} m(z)^T \otimes (\mu + \Sigma z)] + (k-1)[\nabla^{k-2} m(z)^T \otimes \Sigma]\}$.

    Thus, we have proved theorem 1.

    The particular value here of the corollary is that it expresses Gaussian moments in the same gradient form of matrix derivatives that is used in the perturbation solution equations in Section 3. From an analytic standpoint, any arrangement of elements of matrix derivatives is equally acceptable. However, in order to derive useful matrix-algebraic solution equations, the disturbance moments must be expressed compatibly with matrix derivatives in the perturbation equations.

3. PERTURBATION SOLUTION OF THE INFINITE-HORIZON LQEG PROBLEM.

We now focus exclusively on the N = ∞ problem and express (1.1) to (1.4) more compactly.

Using the feedback-control rule (1.2) to eliminate the control vector u and restating the disturbance as $\theta\varepsilon_t$, where $\theta \geq 0$ is a scalar parameter, we write the state law of motion, (1.1), in the closed-loop form

(3.1) $x_t = \Phi x_{t-1} + \theta\varepsilon_t,$

where $\Phi = F_0 + G_0 P_0$ is the closed-loop matrix. The perturbation method produces an approximate Taylor-series solution of the stochastic LQEG problem (henceforth, "stochastic solution"), centered on the exact solution of the nonstochastic LQEG problem (henceforth, "nonstochastic solution"). When $\theta = 0$, the LQEG problem is nonstochastic. In the perturbation method, as θ goes from zero to a positive value it "extrapolates" the nonstochastic solution to an approximate stochastic solution. When $\theta > 0$ but $\neq 1$, the original parameterization is maintained by rescaling Σ as Σ/θ.

For simplicity, we drop the time subscript. Specifically, we write x_{t-1}, ε_t, and E_{t-1} as x, ε, and E. Then, for $N = \infty$, we express (1.4) in the manner of the Bellman equation of dynamic progamming, as

(3.2) $g(x) = f(x) Eg(\Phi x + \theta\varepsilon)^\delta,$

where $f(x) = \exp[-(1/2)x^T Q x]$ and $Q = P_0^T R_0 P_0 + P_0^T S_0 + S_0^T P_0 + Q_0$, so that $g(x) = J(x,\infty)$. For given values of x and the parameters, hence, for given $f(x)$, Φ, θ, and Σ/θ, the $g(x)$ function which solves (3.2) is the stochastic solution. Hansen and Sargent (1995) consider a related logarithmic form of (3.2).

When $\theta = 0$, (3.2) reduces to

(3.3) $g_0(x) = f(x) g_0(\Phi x).$

Whereas the analytical expression of the stochastic solution is unknown, the nonstochastic solution, $g_0(x)$, which solves (3.3) for given values of x and the parameters, is given by

$$(3.4) \qquad g_0(x) = \exp[-(1/2)x^T Vx],$$

where $V = \sum_{k=0}^{\infty} \delta^k (\Phi^T)^k Q \Phi^k$.

We assumed that the quadratic form in (1.3) is non-negative definite overall and positive definite with respect to u, which implies that Q is positive definite (Q > 0). We now also assume that Φ is a stable matrix, i.e., has all eigenvalues less than one in absolute value. The latter assumption is concisely stated as $\rho(\Phi) < 1$, where $\rho(\Phi)$ denotes the spectral radius of Φ, i.e., the largest absolute eigenvalue of Φ.

Given Q > 0 and $0 < \delta \leq 1$, $\rho(\Phi) < 1$ is sufficient for V to exist (be finite) and Q > 0 implies V > 0. By writing $V = Q + \delta\Phi^T[Q + \delta\Phi^T Q\Phi + \delta^2(\Phi^T)^2 Q\Phi^2 + ...]\Phi$ and noting that the expression in brackets is the same as V, we see that $V = \Phi^T V\Phi + Q$. Then, vectorizing this equation using rule (A.3), we obtain

$$(3.5) \qquad \text{vec}(V) = [I_{n^2} - \delta(\Pi_2 \otimes \Phi^T)]^{-1}\text{vec}(Q),$$

where I_{n^2} denotes the $n^2 \times n^2$ identity matrix. Because $0 < \delta \leq 1$, the assumption $\rho(\Phi) < 1$ implies $\delta\rho(\Pi_2 \otimes \Phi) < 1$, hence, that $I_{n^2} - \delta(\Pi_2 \otimes \Phi^T)$ is nonsingular.

Our objective is to compute the 4th-order approximate solution of the infinite-horizon problem without discounting ($\delta = 1$),

$$(3.6) \qquad \hat{g}(x) = g_0 + \nabla g_0(x-x_0) + (1/2)(x-x_0)^T \nabla^2 g_0(x-x_0)$$

$$+ (1/6)[\Pi_2 \otimes (x-x_0)^T]\nabla^3 g_0(x-x_0) + (1/24)[\Pi_3 \otimes (x-x_0)^T]\nabla^4 g_0(x-x_0),$$

where x_0 is any value of the state vector and $g_0 = g(x_0)$, ..., $\nabla^4 g_0 = \nabla^4 g(x_0)$. We restrict the discussion to the undiscounted problem for the sake of brevity. The discounted problem is treated in exactly the same way but involves considerably more algebra.

Because the perturbation method treats θ as a state variable, we define the current and next period's augmented state vectors as $z = (x^T, \theta)^T$ and $z' = x^T \Phi^T + \theta \varepsilon^T, \theta)^T$, and write (3.2) as

$$(3.7) \qquad g^*(z) = f(x) E g^*(z')^\delta .$$

The 4th-order approximation of $g^*(z)$ is

$$(3.8) \qquad \hat{g}^*(z) = g_0^* + \nabla g_0^* (z-z_o) + (1/2)(z-z_o)^T \nabla^2 g_0^* (z-z_o)$$

$$+ (1/6)[\Pi_2 \otimes (z-z_o)^T] \nabla^3 g_0^* (z-z_o) + (1/24)[\Pi_3 \otimes (z-z_o)^T] \nabla^4 g_0^* (z-z_o),$$

where $z_0 = (x_0^T, 0)^T$ and $g_0^* = g^*(z_0)$, ..., $\nabla^4 g_0^* = \nabla^4 g^*(z_0)$.

The perturbation method proceeds as follows: (1) we set $\delta = 1$ and differentiate (3.7) four times in succession with respect to z; (2) we convert the differential form equations into gradient form; (3) we match up coefficients of like powers of elements of dz, which indicates solution equations for g_0^*, ..., $\nabla^4 g_0^*$; (4) we set $\theta = 1$ in (3.8), and consolidate terms into the form of (3.6).

In the following four subsections, we skip most steps in the derivations because including them all would make the paper unbearably long. Full notes on the derivations are available from the authors. However, most steps are elementary, direct or inverse, applications of the vectorization rule (A.3). The direct applications of (A.3) are based on the observations that a scalar is an example of a column vector and that a column vector equals the vectorization of itself. The steps rely mostly on rules (A.3), (A.19), and (A.20), and are used without explicit referencing. The solution equations for ∇g_0^*, ..., $\nabla^4 g_0^*$ derived in this section require $\nabla f(x)$, ..., $\nabla f^4(x)$ as input values. The equations for computing these gradients are derived in appendix B. We use the fact that odd moments of the normally distributed disturbance vector are zero. Finally, for brevity, we write the undiscounted (3.7) as $g^* = f E g^{*\prime}$, and its differentials correspondingly.

3.1. FIRST-ORDER PERTURBATION-SOLUTION EQUATIONS.

Setting $\delta = 1$ and differentiating (3.7) with respect to z, we obtain

(3.9) $dg^* = dfEg^{*\prime} + fEdg^{*\prime}$.

Corresponding to the partition $dz = (dx^T, d\theta)^T$, the columns of the gradient of g^* partition as $\nabla g^* = [\nabla g_1^*, \nabla g_2^*]$. Then, writing the differentials in terms of their gradients and evaluating expectations, we obtain

(3.10) $\nabla g_1^* dx + \nabla g_2^* d\theta = [g^{*\prime} \nabla f + f \nabla g_1^* \Phi] dx + f \nabla g_2^* d\theta$.

Because (3.10) holds for all dx and $d\theta$, we can drop dx and $d\theta$ and obtain

(3.11) $\nabla g_1^* = \nabla g_1^* f\Phi + g^{*\prime} \nabla f$,

(3.12) $\nabla g_2^* = f \nabla g_2^*$.

Note that the ∇g_1^*'s on the left and right sides of (3.11) are identical and evaluated at $z_0 = (x_0^T, 0)^T$, even though they, respectively, stem from g^* and $g^{*\prime}$. The reason is that applying the chain rule of differentiation and evaluating the expectation in (3.9) implements the prime in $dg^{*\prime}$, so that it can be omitted from (3.10) to (3.12) and all derivatives of g^* are evaluated at z_0. The same thing happens in the higher-order perturbation equations. By contrast, the prime stays on $g^{*\prime}$, which is evaluated at z_0 as $g_0(\Phi x_0) = \exp[-(1/2) x_0^T \Phi^T V \Phi x_0]$.

The maintained assumptions, $Q > 0$ and $\rho(\Phi) < 1$, imply that $f < 1$ and $f\rho(\Phi)^k < 1$, hence, that $I_{n^k} - f(\Pi_k \otimes \Phi^T)$ is invertible, for $k = 0, 1, 2, \dots$. Generalizing this section's results, we would see that the invertibility of $I_{n^k} - f(\Pi_k \otimes \Phi^T)$, for $k = 0, 1, \dots, K$, is sufficient and necessary for the existence and uniqueness of the coefficients $g_0^*, \dots, \nabla^K g_0^*$ of the Kth-order approximate solution.

At this point, given that $I_n - f\Phi$ is invertible, (3.11) and (3.12) imply

(3.13) $\nabla g_1^* = g^{*\prime} \nabla f [I_n - f\Phi]^{-1}$, and $\nabla g_2^* = 0_{1\times 1}$.

3.2. SECOND-ORDER PERTURBATION-SOLUTION EQUATIONS.

Differentiating (3.9) with respect to z, we obtain

$$(3.14) \quad d^2g^* = d^2fEg^{*\prime} + 2dfEdg^{*\prime} + fEd^2g^{*\prime}.$$

Corresponding to the partition $dz = (dx^T, d\theta)^T$, the rows and columns of the 2nd-order gradient of g^* partition as

$$(3.15) \quad \nabla^2 g^* = \begin{bmatrix} \nabla^2 g_{11}^* & \nabla^2 g_{12}^* \\ \nabla^2 g_{21}^* & \nabla^2 g_{22}^* \end{bmatrix}.$$

Theoretically, $\nabla^2 g^*$ is symmetric because cross-partial derivatives of g^* are equal. However, practically, we require only that $(z-z_o)^T \nabla^2 g^* (z-z_o)$ is correct regardless of the structure of $\nabla^2 g^*$. That is, a quadratic form can be defined variously, in terms of a symmetric matrix, an upper or lower triangular matrix, or one with no particular pattern. The perturbation method produces n linear restrictions for determining the 2n elements of $\nabla^2 g_{21}^*$ and $\nabla^2 g_{12}^*$, so that n additional linear restrictions must be introduced to determine $\nabla^2 g_{21}^*$ and $\nabla^2 g_{12}^*$ uniquely. The simplest restrictions are $\nabla^2 g_{21}^* = 0_{1\times n}$ or $\nabla^2 g_{12}^* = 0_{n\times 1}$. Arbitrarily, we choose $\nabla^2 g_{21}^* = 0_{1\times n}$.

Then, writing the differentials in (3.14) in terms of their gradients, imposing the previous zero solution ($\nabla g_2^* = 0_{1\times 1}$) and the current zero restriction ($\nabla^2 g_{21}^* = 0_{1\times n}$), vectorizing terms, and evaluating expectations, we obtain

$$(3.16) \quad (\Pi_2 \otimes dx^T)\,\text{vec}(\nabla^2 g_{11}^*) + dx^T d\theta\, \nabla^2 g_{12}^* + (d\theta)^2 \nabla^2 g_{22}^*$$

$$= (\Pi_2 \otimes dx^T)[\text{vec}(g^{*\prime}\nabla^2 f + 2\nabla f^T \nabla g_1^* \Phi) + f(\Pi_2 \otimes \Phi^T)\,\text{vec}(\nabla^2 g_{11}^*)]$$

$$+ dx^T d\theta f \Phi^T \nabla^2 g_{12}^* + (d\theta)^2[f\,\text{vec}(\Sigma)^T \text{vec}(\nabla^2 g_{11}^*) + f\nabla^2 g_{22}^*],$$

where the first term in the second brackets on the right side of the equation is obtained from $E\varepsilon^T \nabla^2 g_{11}^* \varepsilon = E\text{vec}(\varepsilon^T \otimes \varepsilon^T)\text{vec}(\nabla^2 g_{11}^*) = \text{vec}(\Sigma)^T\text{vec}(\nabla^2 g_{11}^*)$.

Because (3.16) holds for all dx and $d\theta$, we can drop dx and $d\theta$ and obtain

$$(3.17) \qquad \text{vec}(\nabla^2 g_{11}^*) = f(\Pi_2 \otimes \Phi^T)\text{vec}(\nabla^2 g_{11}^*) + \text{vec}(g^{*\prime}\nabla^2 f + 2\nabla f^T \nabla g_1^* \Phi),$$

$$(3.18) \qquad \nabla^2 g_{12}^* = f\Phi^T \nabla^2 g_{12}^*,$$

$$(3.19) \qquad \nabla^2 g_{22}^* = f\nabla^2 g_{22}^* + f\text{vec}(\Sigma)^T\text{vec}(\nabla^2 g_{11}^*).$$

Then, given that $I_{n_k} - f(\Pi_k \otimes \Phi^T)$ is invertible for $k = 0, 1, 2$, (3.17) to (3.19) imply

$$(3.20) \qquad \text{vec}(\nabla^2 g_{11}^*) = [I_{n^2} - f(\Pi_2 \otimes \Phi^T)]^{-1}\text{vec}(g^{*\prime}\nabla^2 f + 2\nabla f^T \nabla g_1^* \Phi),$$

$$(3.21) \qquad \nabla^2 g_{22}^* = f(1 - f)^{-1}\text{vec}(\Sigma)^T\text{vec}(\nabla^2 g_{11}^*),$$

and $\nabla^2 g_{12}^* = 0_{n\times 1}$.

3.3. THIRD-ORDER PERTURBATION-SOLUTION EQUATIONS.

Differentiating (3.14) with respect to z, we obtain

$$(3.22) \qquad d^3 g^* = d^3 f E g^{*\prime} + 3d^2 f E dg^{*\prime} + 3df E d^2 g^{*\prime} + f E d^3 g^{*\prime}.$$

Corresponding to the partitions $\Pi_2 \otimes z^T = (\Pi_2 \otimes dx^T, dx^T d\theta, dx^T d\theta, (d\theta)^2)$ and $dz = (dx^T, d\theta)^T$, the rows and columns of the 3rd-order gradient of g^* partition as

$$(3.23) \qquad \nabla^3 g^* = \begin{bmatrix} \nabla^3 g_{11}^* & \nabla^3 g_{12}^* \\ \nabla^3 g_{21}^* & \nabla^3 g_{22}^* \\ \nabla^3 g_{31}^* & \nabla^3 g_{32}^* \\ \nabla^3 g_{41}^* & \nabla^3 g_{42}^* \end{bmatrix}.$$

Considerations of redundancy that led us to set $\nabla^2 g_{21}^* = 0_{1 \times n}$ now lead us to set $\nabla^3 g_{21}^* = \nabla^3 g_{31}^* = 0_{n \times n}$, $\nabla^3 g_{41}^* = 0_{1 \times n}$, and $\nabla^3 g_{32}^* = 0_{n \times 1}$.

Then, writing the differentials in (3.22) in terms of their gradients, imposing previous and current zero restrictions and zero solutions, vectorizing terms, and evaluating expectations, we obtain

$$(3.24) \qquad (\Pi_3 \otimes dx^T) \operatorname{vec}(\nabla^3 g_{11}^*) + (\Pi_2 \otimes dx^T) d\theta \nabla^3 g_{12}^* + dx^T (d\theta)^2 \nabla^3 g_{22}^* + (d\theta)^3 \nabla^3 g_{42}^*$$

$$= (\Pi_3 \otimes dx^T) \{ f(\Pi_3 \otimes \Phi^T) \operatorname{vec}(\nabla^3 g_{11}^*) + \operatorname{vec}[g^{*\prime} \nabla^3 f + 3(\Phi^T \nabla g_1^{*\,T} \otimes \nabla^2 f)$$

$$+ 3(\Phi^T \nabla^2 g_{11}^* \Phi \otimes \nabla f^T)] \} + (\Pi_2 \otimes dx^T) d\theta f(\Pi_2 \otimes \Phi^T) \nabla^3 g_{12}^*$$

$$+ dx^T (d\theta)^2 \{ f\Phi^T \nabla^3 g_{22}^* + 3 \nabla f^T \operatorname{vec}(\Sigma)^T \operatorname{vec}(\nabla^2 g_{11}^*) + 3 \nabla f^T \nabla^2 g_{22}^*$$

$$+ f\Phi^T \nabla^3 g_{11}^{*\,T} \operatorname{vec}(\Sigma) + f[\operatorname{vec}(\Sigma)^T \otimes \Phi^T](K_{n,n^2} + I_{n^3}) \operatorname{vec}(\nabla^3 g_{11}^*) \}$$

$$+ (d\theta)^3 [f \nabla^3 g_{42}^* + f \operatorname{vec}(\Sigma)^T \nabla^3 g_{12}^*].$$

The last term in (3.24), involving the permutation matrix, K_{n,n^2}, is derived using (A.5).

Because (3.24) holds for all dx and $d\theta$, we can drop dx and $d\theta$ and obtain

$$(3.25) \qquad \operatorname{vec}(\nabla^3 g_{11}^*) = f(\Pi_3 \otimes \Phi^T) \operatorname{vec}(\nabla^3 g_{11}^*) + \operatorname{vec}[g^{*\prime} \nabla^3 f + 3(\Phi^T \nabla g_1^{*\,T} \otimes \nabla^2 f)$$

$$+ 3(\Phi^T \nabla^2 g_{11}^* \Phi \otimes \nabla f^T)],$$

(3.26) $\quad \nabla^3 g_{12}^* = f(\Pi_2 \otimes \Phi^T) \nabla^3 g_{12}^*,$

(3.27) $\quad \nabla^3 g_{22}^* = f\Phi^T \nabla^3 g_{22}^* + 3\nabla f^T \text{vec}(\Sigma)^T \text{vec}(\nabla^2 g_{11}^*) + 3\nabla f^T \nabla^2 g_{22}^* + f\Phi^T \nabla^3 g_{11}^{*T} \text{vec}(\Sigma)$

$$+ f[\text{vec}(\Sigma)^T \otimes \Phi^T](K_{n,n^2} + I_{n^3}) \text{vec}(\nabla^3 g_{11}^*),$$

(3.28) $\quad \nabla^3 g_{42}^* = f \nabla^3 g_{42}^* + f\text{vec}(\Sigma)^T \nabla^3 g_{12}^*.$

Then, given that $I_{n^k} - f(\Pi_k \otimes \Phi^T)$ is invertible for $k = 0, 1, 2, 3$, (3.25) to (3.28) imply

(3.29) $\quad \text{vec}(\nabla^3 g_{11}^*) = [I_{n^3} - f(\Pi_3 \otimes \Phi^T)]^{-1} \text{vec}[g^{*\prime} \nabla^3 f + 3(\Phi^T \nabla g_1^{*T} \otimes \nabla^2 f)$

$$+ 3(\Phi^T \nabla^2 g_{11}^* \Phi \otimes \nabla f^T)],$$

(3.30) $\quad \nabla^3 g_{22}^* = [I_n - f\Phi^T]^{-1}\{3\nabla f^T \text{vec}(\Sigma)^T \text{vec}(\nabla^2 g_{11}^*) + 3\nabla f^T \nabla^2 g_{22}^* + f\Phi^T \nabla^3 g_{11}^{*T} \text{vec}(\Sigma)$

$$+ f[\text{vec}(\Sigma)^T \otimes \Phi^T](K_{n,n^2} + I_{n^3}) \text{vec}(\nabla^3 g_{11}^*)\},$$

$\nabla^3 g_{12}^* = 0_{n^2 \times 1}$, and $\nabla^3 g_{42} = 0_{1 \times 1}$.

3.4. FOURTH-ORDER SOLUTION EQUATIONS.

Differentiating (3.22) with respect to z, we obtain

(3.31) $\quad d^4 g^* = d^4 f E g^{*\prime} + 4d^3 f E d g^{*\prime} + 6d^2 f E d^2 g^{*\prime} + 4df E d^3 g^{*\prime} + f E d^4 g^{*\prime}.$

Corresponding to the partitions $\Pi_3 \otimes z^T = (\Pi_3 \otimes dx^T, (\Pi_2 \otimes dx^T)d\theta, (\Pi_2 \otimes dx^T)d\theta, dx^T(d\theta)^2, (\Pi_2 \otimes dx^T)d\theta, dx^T(d\theta)^2, dx^T(d\theta)^2, (d\theta)^3)$ and $dz = (dx^T, d\theta)^T$, the rows and columns of the 4th-order gradient of g^* partition as

(3.32) $\quad \nabla^4 g^{*T} =$

$$\begin{bmatrix} {}^4g_{11}^{*\ T}\nabla & {}^4g_{21}^{*\ T}\nabla & {}^4g_{31}^{*\ T}\nabla & {}^4g_{41}^{*\ T}\nabla & {}^4g_{51}^{*\ T}\nabla & {}^4g_{61}^{*\ T}\nabla & \nabla^4g_{71}^{*\ T} & \nabla^4g_{81}^{*\ T} \\ {}^4g_{12}^{*\ T}\nabla & {}^4g_{22}^{*\ T}\nabla & {}^4g_{32}^{*\ T}\nabla & {}^4g_{42}^{*\ T}\nabla & {}^4g_{52}^{*\ T}\nabla & {}^4g_{62}^{*\ T}\nabla & \nabla^4g_{72}^{*\ T} & \nabla^4g_{82}^{*\ T} \end{bmatrix}.$$

As before, considerations of redundancy lead us to set $\nabla^4g_{21}^* = \nabla^4g_{31}^* = \nabla^4g_{51}^* = 0_{n^2\times n}$, $\nabla^4g_{41}^* = \nabla^4g_{61}^* = \nabla^4g_{71}^* = 0_{n\times n}$, $\nabla^4g_{32}^* = \nabla^4g_{52}^* = 0_{n^2\times 1}$, $\nabla^4g_{62}^* = \nabla^4g_{72}^* = 0_{n\times 1}$, and $\nabla^4g_{81}^* = 0_{1\times n}$.

Then, writing the differentials in (3.31) in terms of their gradients, imposing previous and current zero restrictions and zero solutions, vectorizing terms, and evaluating expectations, we obtain

(3.33) $(\Pi_4\otimes dx^T)\text{vec}(\nabla^4g_{11}^*) + (\Pi_3\otimes dx^T)d\theta\nabla^4g_{12}^* + (\Pi_2\otimes dx^T)(d\theta)^2\nabla^4g_{22}^*$

$+ dx^T(d\theta)^3\nabla^4g_{42}^* + (d\theta)^4\nabla^4g_{82}^* = (\Pi_4\otimes dx^T)\{f(\Pi_4\otimes\Phi^T)\text{vec}(\nabla^4g_{11}^*)$

$+ \text{vec}[g^{*\prime}\nabla^4f + 4(\Phi^T\nabla g_1^{*\ T}\otimes\nabla^3f) + 6(\Phi^T\nabla^2g_{11}^*\Phi\otimes\nabla^2f^T)$

$+ 4(\nabla f^T\otimes\text{vec}((\Pi_2\otimes\Phi^T)\nabla^3g_{11}\Phi))]\} + (\Pi_3\otimes dx^T)d\theta f(\Pi_3\otimes\Phi^T)\nabla^4g_{12}^*$

$+ (\Pi_2\otimes dx^T)(d\theta)^2\{f(\Pi_2\otimes\Phi^T)\nabla^4g_{22}^* + 6[\text{vec}(\Sigma)^T\text{vec}(\nabla^2g_{11}^*) + \nabla^2g_{22}^*]\text{vec}(\nabla^2f)$

$+ 4[(\text{vec}(\Sigma)^T\otimes\Phi^T)(K_{n,n^2}+I_{n^3})\text{vec}(\nabla^3g_{11}^*)\otimes\nabla f^T]$

$+ 4[\Phi^T\nabla^3g_{11}^{*\ T}\text{vec}(\Sigma)\otimes\nabla f^T] + 4[\Phi^T\nabla^3g_{22}^*\otimes\nabla f^T]$

$+ f[(\text{vec}(\Sigma)^T\otimes(\Pi_2\Phi^T))(K_{n,n^3}+K_{n^2,n^2}+I_{n^4})\text{vec}(\nabla^4g_{11}^*)]$

$+ f[(\Phi^T\otimes\text{vec}(\Sigma)^T\otimes\Phi^T)((K_{n,n}\otimes I_{n^2})+(I_{n^2}\otimes K_{n,n})+I_{n^4})\text{vec}(\nabla^4g_{11}^*)]\}$

$+ dx^T(d\theta)^3\{f\Phi^T\nabla^4g_{42} + f(\text{vec}(\Sigma)^T\otimes\Phi^T)(2K_{n,n^2}+I_{n^3})\nabla^4g_{12}^*\}$

$+ (d\theta)^4\{f\nabla^4g_{82}^* + 3f\text{vec}(\Sigma\otimes\Sigma)^T\text{vec}(\nabla^4g_{11}^*) + f\text{vec}(\Sigma)^T\nabla^4g_{22}^*\}.$

In (3.33), terms involving the permutation matrices, K, are derived using (A.5). Because (3.33) holds for all dx and dθ, we can drop dx and dθ and obtain

(3.34) $\text{vec}(\nabla^4 g_{11}^*) = f(\Pi_4 \otimes \Phi^T)\text{vec}(\nabla^4 g_{11}^*) + \text{vec}\{g^{*\prime}\nabla^4 f + 4(\Phi^T \nabla g_1^{*T} \otimes \nabla^3 f)$

$+ 6(\Phi^T \nabla^2 g_{11}^* \Phi \otimes \nabla^2 f^T) + 4[\nabla f^T \otimes \text{vec}((\Pi_2 \otimes \Phi^T)\nabla^3 g_{11}\Phi)]\},$

(3.35) $\nabla^4 g_{12}^* = f(\Pi_3 \otimes \Phi^T)\nabla^4 g_{12}^*,$

(3.36) $\nabla^4 g_{22}^* = f(\Pi_2 \otimes \Phi^T)\nabla^4 g_{22}^* + 6[\text{vec}(\Sigma)^T \text{vec}(\nabla^2 g_{11}^*) + \nabla^2 g_{22}^*]\text{vec}(\nabla^2 f)$

$+ 4[(\text{vec}(\Sigma)^T \otimes \Phi^T)(K_{n,n^2} + I_{n^3})\text{vec}(\nabla^3 g_{11}^*) \otimes \nabla f^T]$

$+ 4[\Phi^T \nabla^3 g_{11}^{*T}\text{vec}(\Sigma) \otimes \nabla f^T] + 4[\Phi^T \nabla^3 g_{22}^* \otimes \nabla f^T]$

$+ f[(\text{vec}(\Sigma)^T \otimes (\Pi_2 \Phi^T))(K_{n,n^3} + K_{n^2,n^2} + I_{n^4})\text{vec}(\nabla^4 g_{11}^*)],$

$+ f[(\Phi^T \otimes \text{vec}(\Sigma)^T \otimes \Phi^T)((K_{n,n} \otimes I_{n^2}) + (I_{n^2} \otimes K_{n,n}) + I_{n^4})\text{vec}(\nabla^4 g_{11}^*)]$

(3.37) $\nabla^4 g_{42}^* = f\Phi^T \nabla^4 g_{42} + f(\text{vec}(\Sigma)^T \otimes \Phi^T)(2K_{n,n^2} + I_{n^3})\nabla^4 g_{12}^*,$

(3.38) $\nabla^4 g_{82}^* = f\nabla^4 g_{82}^* + 3f\text{vec}(\Sigma \otimes \Sigma)^T \text{vec}(\nabla^4 g_{11}^*) + f\text{vec}(\Sigma)^T \nabla^4 g_{22}^*.$

Then, given that $I_{n^k} - f(\Pi_k \otimes \Phi^T)$ is invertible for k = 0, 1, 2, 3, 4, (3.34) to (3.38) imply

(3.39) $\text{vec}(\nabla^4 g_{11}^*) = [I_{n^4} - f(\Pi_4 \otimes \Phi^T)]^{-1}\text{vec}\{g^{*\prime}\nabla^4 f + 4(\Phi^T \nabla g_1^{*T} \otimes \nabla^3 f)$

$+ 6(\Phi^T \nabla^2 g_{11}^* \Phi \otimes \nabla^2 f^T) + 4[\nabla f^T \otimes \text{vec}((\Pi_2 \otimes \Phi^T)\nabla^3 g_{11}\Phi)]\},$

$$(3.40) \quad \nabla^4 g_{22}^* = [I_{n^2} - f(\Pi_2 \otimes \Phi^T)]^{-1} \{6[vec(\Sigma)^T vec(\nabla^2 g_{11}^*) + \nabla^2 g_{22}^*] vec(\nabla^2 f)$$

$$+ 4[(vec(\Sigma)^T \otimes \Phi^T)(K_{n,n^2} + I_{n^3}) vec(\nabla^3 g_{11}^*) \otimes \nabla f^T]$$

$$+ 4[\Phi^T \nabla^3 g_{11}^{*T} vec(\Sigma) \otimes \nabla f^T] + 4[\Phi^T \nabla^3 g_{22}^* \otimes \nabla f^T]$$

$$+ f[(vec(\Sigma)^T \otimes (\Pi_2 \Phi^T))(K_{n,n^3} + K_{n^2,n^2} + I_{n^4}) vec(\nabla^4 g_{11}^*)],$$

$$+ f[(\Phi^T \otimes vec(\Sigma)^T \otimes \Phi^T)((K_{n,n} \otimes I_{n^2}) + (I_{n^2} \otimes K_{n,n}) + I_{n^4}) vec(\nabla^4 g_{11}^*)]\}$$

$$(3.41) \quad \nabla^4 g_{82}^* = f(1 - f)^{-1}[3vec(\Sigma \otimes \Sigma)^T vec(\nabla^4 g_{11}^*) + vec(\Sigma)^T \nabla^4 g_{22}^*],$$

$$\nabla^4 g_{12}^* = 0_{n^3 \times 1}, \text{ and } \nabla^4 g_{42}^* = 0_{n \times 1}.$$

3.5 SUMMARY OF SOLUTION EQUATIONS.

After imposing zero restrictions and zero solutions, (3.8) reduces to

$$(3.42) \quad \hat{g}^*(x,\theta) = g_0^* + \nabla g_1^*(x-x_0) + (1/2)\{(x-x_0)^T \nabla^2 g_{11}^*(x-x_0) + \nabla^2 g_{22}^* \theta^2\}$$

$$+ (1/6)\{[\Pi_2 \otimes (x-x_0)^T] \nabla^3 g_{11}^*(x-x_0) + (x-x_0)^T \nabla^3 g_{22}^* \theta^2\}$$

$$+ (1/24)\{[\Pi_3 \otimes (x-x_0)^T] \nabla^4 g_{11}^*(x-x_0) + [\Pi_2 \otimes (x-x_0)^T] \nabla^4 g_{22}^* \theta^2 + \nabla^4 g_{82}^* \theta^4\}.$$

Setting $\theta = 1$ and consolidating terms in (3.42), writing the result in the form of (3.6), and matching coefficients with those in (3.6), we obtain

$$(3.43) \quad g_0 = g_0^* + (1/2) \nabla^2 g_{22}^* + (1/24) \nabla^4 g_{82}^*,$$

$$(3.44) \quad \nabla g_0 = \nabla g_1^* + (1/6) \nabla^3 g_{22}^{*T},$$

$$(3.45) \quad \nabla^2 g_0 = \nabla^2 g_{11}^* + (1/24) mat(\nabla^4 g_{22}^*),$$

(3.46) $\nabla^3 g_0 = \nabla^3 g_{11}^*$,

(3.47) $\nabla^4 g_0 = \nabla^4 g_{11}^*$,

where $\mathrm{mat}(\nabla^4 g_{22}^*)$ denotes the unvectorization of $\nabla^4 g_{22}^*$ to an n×n matrix, $g_0^* = \exp[-(1/2)x_0^\mathsf{T} V x_0]$ and ∇g_1^*, $\nabla^2 g_{11}^*$, $\nabla^2 g_{22}^*$, $\nabla^3 g_{11}^*$, $\nabla^3 g_{22}^*$, $\nabla^4 g_{11}^*$, $\nabla^4 g_{22}^*$, and $\nabla^4 g_{82}^*$ are given by (3.13), (3.20), (3.21), (3.29), (3.30), (3.39), (3.40), and (3.41).

Extending the solution to the 5th-order adds the equation $\nabla^5 g_0 = \nabla^5 g_{11}^*$ and the terms $(1/120)\nabla^5 g_{16,1}^*$ and $(1/120)\nabla^5 g_{22}^*$ to the right sides of (3.44) and (3.46). In other words, extending a solution's order not only adds new solution equations for higher-order terms but also adds terms to previous lower-order solution equations, that include the effects of higher-order disturbance moments. Thus, there is a double infinity of possible approximate solutions: the coefficients of a solution of any order may include the effects of disturbance moments up to any order.

In the above 4th-order solution, to consider non-Gaussian disturbance distributions that are symmetric about zero, we would need only to replace the 2nd and 4th moments, $\mathrm{vec}(\Sigma)$ and $\mathrm{vec}(\Sigma \otimes \Sigma)$, with the relevant alternatives. For example, without reference to any particular known distribution, we could fatten the tails of the distribution by scaling up $\mathrm{vec}(\Sigma \otimes \Sigma)$ in (3.41), while keeping $\mathrm{vec}(\Sigma)$ constant everywhere. The solution equations must be rederived for distributions that are not symmetric about zero.

4. NUMERICAL EXAMPLE.

This section illustrates the 4th-order solution equations derived in Section 3. The example represents the optimizing behavior of a representative firm in an industry, which maximizes an LQ approximation of its expected present value, subject to its production function, internal adjustment costs, and output demand and input supply conditions (Chen and Zadrozny, 2000a). The problem and its linear feedback solution are given in the standard LQ form by the 2×2 matrices F_0, G_0, R_0, S_0, Q_0, and P_0, specifically,

$$(4.1) \quad F_0 = \begin{bmatrix} .4056 & .0000 \\ .0000 & .4571 \end{bmatrix}, \quad G_0 = \begin{bmatrix} .6587 & .0000 \\ .0000 & .6935 \end{bmatrix}, \quad R_0 = \begin{bmatrix} 44.43 & -44.33 \\ -44.33 & 44.43 \end{bmatrix},$$

$$S_0 = \begin{bmatrix} -.4349 & -.9338 \\ -.4351 & -.9350 \end{bmatrix}, \quad Q_0 = \begin{bmatrix} 1.064 & .8688 \\ .8689 & 2.865 \end{bmatrix}, \quad P_0 = \begin{bmatrix} .1008 & .1961 \\ .1002 & .1857 \end{bmatrix},$$

which imply

$$(4.2) \quad Q = \begin{bmatrix} .8912 & .5189 \\ .5189 & 2.164 \end{bmatrix}, \quad \Phi = \begin{bmatrix} .4720 & .1292 \\ .0695 & .5858 \end{bmatrix}, \quad V = \begin{bmatrix} 1.256 & 1.037 \\ 1.037 & 3.566 \end{bmatrix}.$$

To compute the 4th-order approximate solution of the LQEG problem, we also assume that $\text{vec}(\Sigma) = (1., .5, .5, 1.)^T$ and evaluate the solution equations at $x_0 = (\sqrt{.5}, \sqrt{.5})^T \cong (.7071, .7071)^T$. Thus, we obtain the following values for the coefficients of 4th-order approximate solution,

$$(4.3) \quad g_0 = .0043, \quad \nabla g_1 = [.0021, .0059], \quad \nabla^2 g_0 = \begin{bmatrix} .0049 & .0119 \\ .0081 & .0241 \end{bmatrix},$$

$$\nabla^3 g_0{}^T = \begin{bmatrix} -.2663 & .0356 & .0435 & .0610 \\ .0608 & .0608 & .0784 & .1213 \end{bmatrix},$$

$$\nabla^4 g_0{}^T = \begin{bmatrix} .0390 & .0637 & .0642 & .1110 & .0699 & .1196 & .1217 & .2341 \\ .0622 & .1185 & .1179 & .2334 & .1149 & .2233 & .2244 & .4988 \end{bmatrix}.$$

These results give some sense of the sizes of the coefficients of the 4th-order approximate solution.

5. CONCLUSION.

The paper has derived and illustrated recursions for computing any multivariate Gaussian moment and equations for computing the 4th-order Taylor-series approximation of the objective function of the infinite-horizon LQEG problem. There are several possible extensions of the paper. We could optimize $g(x)$ numerically with respect to the linear feedback matrix, P_0. Of course, we could also do this following Jacobson (1973), by solving an algebraic Riccati equation. It would be interesting to derive and illustrate corresponding results for a non-Gaussian disturbance distribution, say, the fatter-tailed multivariate t distribution. Of course, for a non-Gaussian distribution, the optimal decision rule will usually be nonlinear. In such a case, we should derive and solve equations for simultaneously computing $\hat{g}(x)$ and the approximate optimal nonlinear decision rule, $\hat{P}(x)$, although this possibility would be significantly more complicated than optimizing $\hat{g}(x)$ numerically with respect to P_0. In any of these possibilities, we could consider the discounted problem.

The present perturbation method is different from that of Collard and Juillard (2000) and Sims (2000), in which the stochastic problem is solved by first perturbing the disturbance vector in the nonstochastic version of a problem and, then, accounting for stochastic variation of the disturbances by taking expectations of the nonstochastic perturbation equations. In our experience, this method produces identical 1st- and 2nd-order approximate solutions of stochastic problems, with equivalent effort, but, for higher-order solutions of multivariate stochastic problems, produces intractable solution equations. For this reason, we follow Fleming (1971) and Fleming and Souganidis (1986) and account for stochastic variation in terms of the perturbation parameter θ. Fleming's method is also applied by Anderson and Hansen (1996), Judd (1998), and Chen and Zadrozny (2000b).

APPENDIX A: DEFINITIONS AND RULES OF MATRIX DIFFERENTIATION.

A.1. DEFINITIONS OF MATRIX DERIVATIVES.

Let $A(x) \in \mathbf{D}^k$: $\mathbf{R}^n \rightarrow \mathbf{R}^{p \times q}$ be a K-times differentiable p×q matrix function of the n-vector x. $A(x)$ could be a function of the matrix $X \in \mathbf{R}^{k \times m}$, such that x = vec(X), where vec(X) is the columnwise vectorization of a matrix. We consider derivatives of elements of A with respect to elements of x in three forms: the ∂ or partial derivative form, the d or differential form, and the ∇ or gradient form.

For $k = 1, \ldots, K$ and $i_1, \ldots, i_k \in \{1, \ldots, n\}$, we define $\partial^k_{i_1 \cdots i_k} A \in \mathbf{R}^{p \times q}$ by

$$
\text{(A.1)} \qquad \partial^k_{i_1 \cdots i_k} A = \begin{bmatrix} \dfrac{\partial^k A_{11}}{\partial x_{i_1} \cdots \partial x_{i_k}} & \cdots & \dfrac{\partial^k A_{1q}}{\partial x_{i_1} \cdots \partial x_{i_k}} \\ \vdots & & \vdots \\ \dfrac{\partial^k A_{p1}}{\partial x_{i_1} \cdots \partial x_{i_k}} & \cdots & \dfrac{\partial^k A_{pq}}{\partial x_{i_1} \cdots \partial x_{i_k}} \end{bmatrix},
$$

as the <u>partial derivative form</u> of k-th order partial derivatives of the elements of A with respect to $x_{i_1}, \ldots, x_{i_k}$.

The <u>differential form</u> associated with (A.1) is

$$
\text{(A.2)} \qquad d^k A = \sum_{i_1=1}^{n} \cdots \sum_{i_k=1}^{n} \partial_{i_1 \cdots i_k} A \, dx_{i_1} \times \times \times dx_{i_k},
$$

where the dx_i's are small (strictly, infinitesimal) increments to the elements of $x = (x_1, \ldots, x_n)^T$.

The <u>gradient form</u> associated with (A.1) and (A.2) can now be built up recursively, starting with $k = 1$. Because there is no generally accepted terminology for higher-order derivatives of matrix-valued functions, such as gradient and Hessian for scalar-valued functions or Jacobian for vector-valued functions, we call the matrix representations of kth-order derivatives of matrix functions "kth-order gradients."

Three rules are needed for vectorizing and permuting matrix elements. First,

(A.3) $\text{vec}(ABC) = [C^T \otimes A]\text{vec}(B),$

where A, B, and C are matrices conformable to the matrix product ABC and $\otimes$ denotes the Kronecker matrix product (Magnus and Neudecker, 1988, p.30).

In sections 2 and 3, we apply (A.3) directly and inversely. "Directly" means applying (A.3) from left to right, i.e., expressing the vectorization of ABC as $[C^T \otimes A]\text{vec}(B)$. "Inversely" means applying (A.3) from right to left, i.e., expressing the unvectorization of $[C^T \otimes A]\text{vec}(B)$ as a matrix whose vectorization equals vec(ABC). We denote the inverse or "un" vectorization by mat($\times$) and state its particular dimensions alongside.

Second,

(A.4) $\text{vec}(A \otimes B) = [I_n \otimes (K_{q,m} \otimes I_p)(I_m \otimes \text{vec}(B))]\text{vec}(A)$

$= [(I_n \otimes K_{q,m})(\text{vec}(A) \otimes I_q) \otimes I_p]\text{vec}(B),$

where A and B are m×n and p×q matrices, I_j denotes the j×j identity matrix, and $K_{q,m}$ denotes the qm×qm permutation matrix that maps the vectorization of a q×m matrix to the vectorization of its transpose (Magnus and Neudecker, 1988, p. 48). The definition of $K_{q,m}$ implies $K_{q,m}^T = (K_{q,m})^{-1} = K_{m,q}$.

Third,

(A.5) $(A \otimes b^T)K_{n,p} = b^T \otimes A,$

where A is m×n and b^T is 1×p (Magnus and Neudecker, 1988, p. 47).

In $B = K_{m,n}A$, where A and B are mn×p, $K_{m,n}A$ can be viewed as a permutation operation on the elements of matrix A or as the matrix $K_{m,n}$ that premultiplies the matrix A in the ordinary matrix product. In the first case, consider $B = K_{m,n}A$ as $b_j = K_{m,n}a_j$, for j = 1, ..., p, where a_j and b_j are mn×1 columns of A and B. For each j = 1, ..., p, consider a_j as an m×n matrix, transpose this matrix, and assign its column vectorization to b_j. Thus, we construct $B = K_{m,n}A$. In the second case, consider $K_{m,n} = K_{m,n}I_{mn}$, where I_{mn} is the mn×mn identity matrix. $K_{m,n}$ on the right side of the equality is viewed as the permutation operator, as in the first case, and $K_{m,n}$ on the left side is the result of permuting I_{mn}. Thus, we construct $K_{m,n}$ as a permutation of I_{mn}.

We emphasize that throughout the paper a "vector" or the result of a "vectorization" is a column vector.

A.2. REPRESENTATIONS OF MATRIX DERIVATIVES.

For k = 1, (A.1) and (A.2) become

$$
(A.6) \qquad \partial_k A = \begin{bmatrix} \dfrac{\partial A_{11}}{\partial x_i} & \cdots & \dfrac{\partial A_{1q}}{\partial x_i} \\ \vdots & & \vdots \\ \dfrac{\partial A_{p1}}{\partial x_i} & \cdots & \dfrac{\partial A_{pq}}{\partial x_i} \end{bmatrix} ,
$$

$$
(A.7) \qquad dA = \sum_{i=1}^{n} \partial_i A dx_i .
$$

Note that vectorization, summation, and differentiation operations are commutative, i.e., can be applied in any order. Therefore, we vectorize (A.7), to obtain

$$
(A.8) \qquad \mathrm{vec}(dA) = [\partial_1 \mathrm{vec}(A), \ldots, \partial_n \mathrm{vec}(A)] dx,
$$

where $dx = (dx_1, \ldots, dx_n)^T$, so that

$$
(A.9) \qquad \mathrm{vec}(dA) = \nabla A dx,
$$

$$
(A.10) \qquad \nabla A = [\partial_1 \mathrm{vec}(A), \ldots, \partial_n \mathrm{vec}(A)].
$$

Equations (A.9) and (A.10) relate the ∂, d, and ∇ forms of first-order derivatives of A to each other.

To obtain analogues of (A.9) and (A.10) for k = 2, we differentiate them to obtain

$$
(A.11) \qquad \mathrm{vec}(d^2 A) = d(\nabla A) dx,
$$

$$
(A.12) \qquad d(\nabla A) = [d(\mathrm{vec}(\partial_1 A)), \ldots, d(\mathrm{vec}(\partial_n A))]
$$

$$= \sum_{j=1}^{n} \; [\partial_j(\text{vec}(\partial_1 A)), \; \ldots, \; \partial_j(\text{vec}(\partial_n A))] \, dx_j.$$

Then, we vectorize (A.12) to obtain

$$(A.13) \qquad \text{vec}(d(\nabla A)) = \sum_{j=1}^{n} \begin{bmatrix} \partial_j(\text{vec}(\partial_1 A)) \\ \vdots \\ \partial_j(\text{vec}(\partial_n A)) \end{bmatrix} dx_j = \begin{bmatrix} \partial_1(\text{vec}(\partial_1 A)) & \cdots & \partial_n(\text{vec}(\partial_1 A)) \\ \vdots & & \vdots \\ \partial_1(\text{vec}(\partial_n A)) & \cdots & \partial_n(\text{vec}(\partial_n A)) \end{bmatrix} dx.$$

Then, because $\text{vec}(\nabla A) = \begin{bmatrix} \partial_1(\text{vec}(A)) \\ \vdots \\ \partial_n(\text{vec}(A)) \end{bmatrix} = \begin{bmatrix} \text{vec}(\partial_1 A) \\ \vdots \\ \text{vec}(\partial_n A) \end{bmatrix}$, we obtain

$$(A.14) \qquad \text{vec}(d(\nabla A)) = [\partial_1 \text{vec}(\nabla A), \; \ldots, \; \partial_n \text{vec}(\nabla A)] \, dx.$$

Continuing in this manner for k = 2, ..., K, we obtain

$$(A.15) \qquad \text{vec}(d(\nabla^{k-1} A)) = \nabla^k A \, dx,$$

$$(A.16) \qquad \text{vec}(d^k A) = [(\Pi_{k-1} \otimes dx^T) \otimes I_{pq}] \nabla^k A \, dx,$$

where $\Pi_{k-1} \otimes dx^T$ denotes k-1 successive Kronecker products of dx^T, and

$$(A.17) \qquad \nabla^k A = [\partial_1 \text{vec}(\nabla^{k-1} A), \; \ldots, \; \partial_n \text{vec}(\nabla^{k-1} A)].$$

Applied for k = 1, ..., K, (A.17) recusively organizes gradient form derivatives of A up to order K as matrices. Basically, $\nabla^k A$ is the Jacobian matrix of the vectorization of $\nabla^{k-1} A$.

In this gradient representation of matrix derivatives, the K-term Taylor-series approximation of A(x) at x = x_0 is

$$(A.18) \qquad \text{vec}(\hat{A}(x)) = \sum_{k=0}^{K} \; (1/k!) \text{vec}(\nabla^k A_0)^T \{ [\Pi_k \otimes (x-x_0)] \otimes I_{pq} \},$$

such that $\nabla^k A_0 = \nabla^k A(x_0)$, for $k \geq 1$, and $\nabla^0 A_0 = A(x_0)$.

A.3. DIFFERENTIATION RULES.

Let $A(x) \in \mathbf{D}: \mathbf{R}^n \to \mathbf{R}^p$ and $B(y) \in \mathbf{D}: \mathbf{R}^p \to \mathbf{R}^q$ be differentiable vector functions (or vectorizations of matrix functions). Let $C(x) \in \mathbf{D}: \mathbf{R}^n \to \mathbf{R}^q$ be the differentiable composite vector function $C(x) = B(A(x))$. Then, the gradient form of derivatives of $C(x)$ is given by the <u>chain</u> <u>rule</u> <u>of</u> <u>differentiation</u>,

(A.19) $\nabla C(x) = \nabla B(A) \cdot \nabla A(x)$.

Let $A(x) \in \mathbf{D}: \mathbf{R}^n \to \mathbf{R}^{p \times q}$ and $B(x) \in \mathbf{D}: \mathbf{R}^n \to \mathbf{R}^{p \times q}$ be differentiable matrix functions conformable to the ordinary matrix product $C(x) = A(x) \times B(x)$. Then, the differential form of derivatives of $C(x)$ is given by the <u>product</u> <u>rule</u> <u>of</u> <u>differentiation</u>,

(A.20) $dC(x) = dA(x) \times B(x) + A(x) \times dB(x)$.

Rules (A.19) and (A.20) are quickly proved by elementwise application of the scalar chain rule of differentiation and the scalar product rule of differentiation.

APPENDIX B: INPUT DERIVATIVES FOR PERTURBATION SOLUTION.

This appendix derives equations for computing the first to fourth gradient matrices $\nabla f(x)$, ..., $\nabla^4 f(x)$ of $f(x) = \exp[-(1/2)x^T Q x]$, which are the inputs for computing the 4th-order approximation of the stochastic solution function, $g(x)$. As in Section 3, without further reference, we vectorize scalars, vectors, and matrices using rule (A.3), differentiate expressions using the chain and product rules of differentiation, (A.19) and (A.20), and repeatedly use the fact that $f(x)$ is scalar valued. However, we do reference vectorization rule (A.4) when we use it. In the example in section 4, $f(x)$, ..., $\nabla^4 f(x)$ are evaluated at x_0.

Differentiating $f(x)$, we obtain

$$(B.1) \qquad df(x) = -f(x) x^T Q dx.$$

Then, noting that $df(x) = \nabla f(x) dx$ and dropping dx, we obtain

$$(B.2) \qquad \nabla f(x) = -f(x) x^T Q.$$

Differentiating (B.2), we obtain

$$(B.3) \qquad d(\nabla f(x)) = -df(x) x^T Q - f(x) dx^T Q.$$

Vectorizing (B.3) and eliminating $df(x)$ using (B.1), we obtain $\text{vec}[d(\nabla f(x))] = f(x)(Qxx^T Q + Q)dx$. Then, noting that $\text{vec}[d(\nabla f(x))] = \nabla^2 f(x) dx$ and dropping dx, we obtain

$$(B.4) \qquad \nabla^2 f(x) = f(x)(-Q + Qxx^T Q).$$

Differentiating (B.4), we obtain

$$(B.5) \qquad d(\nabla^2 f(x)) = df(x)(-Q + Qxx^T Q) + f(x) Q(dxx^T + xdx^T) Q.$$

Vectorizing (B.5), we obtain $\text{vec}[d(\nabla^2 f(x))] = \text{vec}(-Q + Qxx^T Q)df(x) + f(x)(Qx \otimes Q)dx + f(x)(Q \otimes Qx)dx$. Then, eliminating $df(x)$ using (B.1), noting that $\text{vec}[d(\nabla^2 f(x))] = \nabla^3 f(x) dx$, and dropping dx, we obtain

$$(B.6) \qquad \nabla^3 f(x) = f(x)[\text{vec}(Q - Qxx^T Q) x^T Q + (Qx \otimes Q) + (Q \otimes Qx)].$$

Differentiating (B.6), we obtain

(B.7) $d(\nabla^3 f(x)) = df(x)[\text{vec}(Q - Qxx^TQ)x^TQ + (Qx \otimes Q) + (Q \otimes Qx)]$

$+ f(x)\{-\text{vec}[Q(dxx^T + xdx^T)Q)]x^TQ + \text{vec}(Q - Qxx^TQ)dx^TQ$

$+ (Qdx \otimes Q) + (Q \otimes Qdx)\}.$

Vectorizing (B.7), we obtain

(B.8) $\text{vec}[d(\nabla^3 f(x))] = \text{vec}[\text{vec}(Q - Qxx^TQ)x^TQ + (Qx \otimes Q) + (Q \otimes Qx)]df(x)$

$- f(x)\{(Qx \otimes I_{n^2})[(Qx \otimes Q) + (Q \otimes Qx)]dx$

$+ [Q \otimes \text{vec}(Q - Qxx^TQ)]dx$

$+ \text{vec}(Qdx \otimes Q) + \text{vec}(Q \otimes Qdx)\},$

where I_{n^2} denotes the $n^2 \times n^2$ identity matrix. Vectorization rule (A.4) implies

(B.9) $\text{vec}(Qdx \otimes Q) = [K_{n,n} \otimes I_n][I_n \otimes \text{vec}(Q)]Qdx,$

(B.10) $\text{vec}(Q \otimes Qdx) = [\text{vec}(Q) \otimes I_n]Qdx,$

because $I_1 = \text{scalar } 1$ and $K_{n1} = K_{1n} = I_n$. Then, using (B.1), (B.9), and (B.10), noting that $\text{vec}[d(\nabla^3 f(x))] = \nabla^4 f(x)dx$, and dropping dx, (B.8) becomes

(B.11) $\nabla^4 f(x) = f(x)\{\text{vec}[\text{vec}(Q - Qxx^TQ)x^TQ + (Qx \otimes Q) + (Q \otimes Qx)]x^TQ$

$- (Qx \otimes I_{n^2})[(Qx \otimes Q) + (Q \otimes Qx)] + [Q \otimes \text{vec}(Q - Qxx^TQ)]$

$+ [K_{n,n} \otimes I_n][I_n \otimes \text{vec}(Q)]Q + [\text{vec}(Q) \otimes I_n]Q\}.$

REFERENCES.

Anderson, E.W. and L.P. Hansen (1996), "Perturbation Methods for Risk-Sensitive Economies," working paper, Department of Economics, University of Chicago, Chicago, IL.

Chen, B. and P.A. Zadrozny (2000a), "Estimated U.S. Manufacturing Capital and Productivity Based on an Estimated Dynamic Economic Model," working paper, Department of Economics, Rutgers University, Camden, NJ.

Chen, B. and P.A. Zadrozny (2000b), "Perturbation Solution of Nonlinear Rational Expectations Models," working paper, presented at the Computational Economics segment of the SITE 2000 summer workshop, Department of Economics, Stanford University, Stanford, CA.

Collard, F. and M. Juillard (2000), "Accuracy of Stochastic Perturbation Methods: The Case of Asset Pricing Models," Journal of Economic Dynamics and Control, forthcoming.

Fleming, W.H. (1971), "Stochastic Control for Small Noise Intensities," SIAM Journal of Control 9: 473-517.

Fleming, W.H. and P.E. Souganidis (1986), "Asymptotic Series and the Method of Vanishing Viscosity," Indiana University Mathematics Journal 35: 425-447.

Hansen, L.P. and T.J. Sargent (1995), "Discounted Linear Exponential Quadratic Gaussian Control," IEEE Transactions on Automatic Control AC-40: 968-971.

Jacobson, D.H. (1973), "Optimal Stochastic Linear Systems with Exponential Performance Criteria and their Relation to Deterministic Differential Games," IEEE Transactions on Automatic Control AC-18: 124-131.

Judd, K.L. (1998), Numerical Methods in Economics, Cambridge, MA: MIT Press.

Karp, L.S. (1985), "Higher Moments in the Linear-Quadratic-Gaussian Problem," Journal of Economic Dynamics and Control 9: 41-54.

Laub, A.J. (1979), "A Schur Method for Solving Algebraic Riccati Equations," IEEE Transactions on Automatic Control 24: 913-921.

MacRae, E.C. (1974), "Matrix Derivatives with an Application to an Adaptive Linear Decision Problem," Annals of Statistics 2: 337-346.

Magnus, J.R. and H. Neudecker (1988), Matrix Differential Calculus with Applications in Statistics and Econometrics, New York, NY: J. Wiley & Sons.

Sims, C.A. (2000), "Second Order Solution of Discrete Time Dynamic Equilibrium Models," working paper, Department of Economics, Princeton University, Princeton, NJ.